THE CF. ⌐⌐ ⌐F ADDICTION

— ✝ —

The CROSS *of* ADDICTION

Reflections on the Stations of the Cross for an *Addicted* World

Edited by

BARRY MATTHEWS

VERITAS

Published 2017 by
Veritas Publications
7–8 Lower Abbey Street
Dublin 1, Ireland

publications@veritas.ie
www.veritas.ie

ISBN 978 1 84730 779 8

Copyright © individual contributors, 2017

10 9 8 7 6 5 4 3 2 1

The Stations of the Cross © Debra Millet – Thinkstock Photos

'Indifference' by GA Studdert-Kennedy on page 43 is taken from *The Unutterable Beauty*. Published by Hodder & Stoughton, 1927.

The material in this publication is protected by copyright law. Except as may be permitted by law, no part of the material may be reproduced (including by storage in a retrieval system) or transmitted in any form or by any means, adapted, rented or lent without the written permission of the copyright owners. Applications for permissions should be addressed to the publisher.

A catalogue record for this book is available from the British Library.

Designed by Lir MacCárthaigh
Cover painting © Sara Kyne
Printed in Ireland by Colorman (Ireland) Ltd, Dublin

Veritas books are printed on paper made from the wood pulp of managed forests. For every tree felled, at least one tree is planted, thereby renewing natural resources.

CONTENTS

— ACKNOWLEDGEMENTS —

It is important to acknowledge the commitment given
by all those who contributed to this publication.

A special word of thanks to Kitty, Damien, David and
Lucy who have offered personal testimonies that give
an insight into addiction from various viewpoints and
which have offered a sense of the reality of the cross
of addiction.

A particular word of thanks to H.E. Archbishop Charles
Brown, Archbishop Eamon Martin and Archbishop
Richard Clarke who have offered much support
and who are involved at many levels in the care of
those who suffer from addiction and those who are
associated with them.

‹ INTRODUCTION ›

WE LIVE IN A society where the cross of addiction
is carried by many – there are both those who are
addicted and those who journey with the addicted
whom they love and care for. We all journey towards
our Calvary in different ways over our lives and at
different times. Calvary can be a point that we are
led to over many years or it can be a quicker process
brought on by a tragedy – either way, it is a moment
when our life is changed and we are forced to react.

The Stations of the Cross offer a way of praying
that assures us that Jesus accompanies each one of us
towards Calvary. By praying the Way of the Cross we
are reminded that Jesus has walked the road before us
and promises us that he is the strength that we need
for the journey.

Many people carry more than one cross; for some
they are so burdened by their crosses that they often
wonder where they will find the physical strength to
carry them further. Jesus felt the burden of his cross –
Jesus fell three times but, with the knowledge of the

love of our heavenly father, he got up and continued on the journey so that we would know that he has walked the difficult path which we face before us.

The Stations of the Cross are a reminder that Jesus accepted the cross and so too must we face up to the difficulties in life. It is in facing up and accepting that we have crosses to carry that we can begin to acknowledge our need for help. The cross was a significant part of Jesus' journey towards the freedom which ultimately we journey towards.

In accepting the cross of addiction – in accepting that the problem even exists and is real – those addicted can move towards the healing that they need. Those who journey with the addicted can, by facing up to the reality of their loved one's addiction, receive a sense of freedom that will allow them to seek the help and assistance they might need.

The strength that is needed to overcome the cross of addiction is spiritual and emotional. The strength needed can also be likened to the physical strength required to carry an actual cross. Like physical strength it is important that emotional and spiritual strength is built up in order that we can bear the weight of the crosses we face.

It is in acknowledging that the cross of addiction is real that those suffering from addiction can begin the process towards managing the real weight of the cross that they bear. Jesus had Simon of Cyrene to assist him carry the cross and so too those with addictions must have a strong support network to ease the moments when the burden increases.

Like any journey there will be pitfalls along the road to recovery, but in time it will seem more manageable – this happens through the supports and strengths that have been built up.

Dark days are real and some even say necessary – Jesus spent three days in hell, addicts and their carers often describe longer periods where they feel like they are in hell! Addicts must know what support will bring them out of the darkness, knowing where to turn to seek those who will bring the light of hope to their lives.

Entering the darkness, those addicted must call on their support network. Jesus fell three times and each time got back up. Knowing that the cross is heavy and one may fall under its weight sometimes, the important thing is not to lose hope. Jesus met his mother and the women of Jerusalem along the 'way of the cross'. These were his family, these were the people who supported him. Sometimes support comes from strangers and, in that moment, they become like family – Jesus on the Cross spoke to his close friend

John telling him that Mary was now his mother too and to Mary he said that John was now her son.

In strengthening the family bonds between those who supported him, Jesus invites us to be strong as a family of faith and to come together to support each other when we are in need.

The route towards Calvary was lined with many people who supported Jesus but also with many people who abused him – many people who hated him. Jesus, in his hour of pain, perhaps feeling the world had united against him, was forced to struggle through. Jesus was given the strength to continue, though his bones were aching, the strength came from knowing that he was going through suffering for others.

When the pain is hardest because of the battle with addiction, or because a loved one is battling addiction, it is important to understand that you are carrying the cross. Accepting the cross will bring those affected by the struggle towards a new life. Suffering is the cross and though the cross is our hope – suffering is our door to eternal hope.

It is okay to say that the cross is our sign of hope but it is important to go further and explain why this is so. The cross is our hope because of the relationship that it represents. Our relationship with Jesus is based on our understanding of how his suffering freed us from an eternal life of darkness. Often our relationship with Jesus needs to be renewed due to a long absence from prayer caused perhaps directly or indirectly by the addiction which has shaped a part of our lives. Our relationship may have been one way traffic – Jesus never stops loving and caring for us; however, sometimes we turn away from him.

We look to Jesus on the cross to see how he reacts when we turn away from him, Jesus is at that moment looking out towards a broken world where some people are happy to see him being tortured and killed and yet Jesus never gives up on us. Jesus holds the key to self-control and it is self-control that will ultimately enable those addicted to overcome even the heaviest of crosses.

The good thief hanging beside Jesus knew that he was in the presence of a man whose very being stood for new life and new hope. By his composure in accepting the cross the thief knew this man was free. The captured thief reached out to Jesus – acknowledging Jesus for who he was, the good thief asked Jesus for forgiveness. By his very cry 'Jesus remember me' he proclaimed his love for Jesus. Jesus promised him eternal joy – freedom from the cross and a life in the presence of Jesus. This promise is available to us all – all we need to do is ask 'Jesus remember me'.

The cross was not all about freedom – hanging on the cross knowing that he was returning home, Jesus still showed his human side. Jesus felt fear – the fear that many addicts feel during detox – the fear that many families fear when their loved one is engaging in the object of the addiction. Jesus in his most powerful of prayers spoke directly to the father from the cross. The words 'My God, My God why have you forsaken me' are words that we can all relate to. We can understand the fear, the anxiety, the despair.

We learn a new way of prayer at this moment of the journey towards a fresh start. We learn from the cross that we can talk to Jesus in our despair, we can talk to Jesus in words that sum up what addiction is for us, the words that explain the feelings of being forsaken, lonely, empty, rejected. We can learn from Jesus on the cross that he feels our pain, for it is for our sake that he is willing to give his life. It is this very relationship with Jesus that gives us hope, our hope pours out from our understanding that he walks with us towards and through our Calvary.

In praying the Stations of the Cross we are transported to the very journey of suffering that Jesus walked. We carry our crosses knowing that Jesus carried a heavy cross so that we will always have him to call on when we need help with our own crosses. Our journeys are unique and so too are our relationships with Jesus. The journey through the Stations of the Cross can help us to reflect upon the paths that we find difficult.

The stations can be prayed as a continuous prayer journey or the reflections can be used as a tool on which to meditate and ponder over individual stations. Whether the stations are prayed in one session or over a period, they still act as a reminder that nobody walks alone when carrying their cross.

The stations as presented here act also as a reminder that there are many people who carry the cross of addiction and many groups and organisations who offer much needed support and care, and they are always available to offer their assistance.

The contributors have written their own experiences of addiction through the lens of the cross and are all closely linked to those suffering with addictions of one kind or another. Many of the major charitable organisations in the area of addiction are represented. The support of these organisations that often work in every corner of Ireland and who are available around the clock is invaluable not only to those affected but to wider society. Those who have given personal testimonies have done so in the hope that others will see that they are not alone in the difficulties that they face. They have written in the hope that their story will be the catalyst for others to seek help and a better life for themselves and those they love.

The stations have been arranged to be prayed as a continuous meditation or alternatively one might reflect on a particular aspect of Jesus' journey to Calvary that has a particular relevance to you on your own spiritual journey.

JESUS IS CONDEMNED TO DEATH

We Adore You, O Christ, and we Praise You —
because by Your Holy Cross, You have Redeemed the World.

Pilate spoke to them again, 'Then what do you wish me to do with this man you call the King of the Jews?' They shouted back, 'Crucify him!' Pilate asked them, 'Why, what evil has he done?' But they shouted all the more, 'Crucify him!' So Pilate, wishing to satisfy the crowd, released Barabbas for them; and after flogging Jesus, he handed him over to be crucified.

Mark 15:12–15

Reflection by
BR KEVIN CROWLEY OFM CAP
Capuchin Day Centre, Dublin

THE FIRST STATION states very starkly that Jesus was condemned to death by crucifixion. Bruised and bleeding, he was to face the arduous road to Calvary. The only sympathetic eyes looking on were those of his mother Mary, Saint John and the women who attended on him during his journeys throughout Palestine. Pilate had condemned an innocent man to death. Unlike Jesus, we cannot claim that we are innocent of wrongdoing. As the Good Thief said, dying on his cross, 'This man has done nothing wrong'. But we have done wrong and we know it. The Good News, however, is that God the Father allows Jesus, the Beloved Son, to be condemned to death 'for us', his brothers and sisters. He took up his cross for us, died for us that we would have life. The suffering and death of Jesus are not pointless and purposeless. In the words of our ancient Creed, 'For our sake he was crucified under Pontius Pilate'.

Often, throughout our lives, we too have had to face difficult situations alone. It seemed our world was crumbling before us because of our weaknesses, our sins, failings and addictions which brought isolation, guilt, helplessness and unhappiness. We had nowhere to go. We had failed everyone – our families, our friends – and we hated ourselves for the shame we had brought on them through our stupidity, ugliness and selfishness. It seemed easier to die than to go on living. We needed help and yet we were too weak and afraid to trust and begin again. Abandoned by all, even by God, or so it seemed, we wanted to die. All seemed lost. We were in despair.

What we didn't know was that our God had not abandoned us and given up on us. He is the one who can give us back our dignity, reaffirm our destiny, and awaken the promise of eternal life and salvation. He sent a good Samaritan to strengthen and lift us up. The presence and kind words of such good Samaritans gave us hope; their patience and willingness to listen to our story gave us strength. We could see the care in their eyes and feel the concern in their words. Such persons introduced us again to our family and friends, helping us to believe again, and to face up to the suffering we had caused them.

Lord Jesus, I thank you for the gentle and loving people you sent into my life to bring about my conversion. The people who prayed for me and persevered with me. I am grateful for their presence in my life. They stood by me, as Mary stood at the foot of the cross when her son was dying. They opened the door to a new life. They helped us limp through that door. They put new heart into us. They helped us to realise that Jesus is never ashamed to call us his brothers and sisters, even though the whole world may despise us and treat us with contempt. Bless them, Lord, for their love and patience. Help all those who struggle with their sinful habits and addictions. Help us to stand by the cross of our brothers and sisters who suffer from addiction without condemning them. Help us to inspire them with the will to fight back against addiction and to find empowerment in their situation. Jesus, grant us your mercy. Amen.

God, grant me the Serenity to accept the things I cannot change,
Courage to change the things I can,
And Wisdom to know the difference.

JESUS CARRIES HIS CROSS

We Adore You, O Christ, and we Praise You —
because by Your Holy Cross, You have Redeemed the World.

Then he handed him over to them to be crucified. So they took Jesus; and carrying the cross by himself, he went out to what is called The Place of the Scull, which in Hebrew is called Golgotha.

John 19:16–17

Reflection by
FR PETER MCVERRY SJ
Founder: The Peter McVerry Trust

HAVING BEEN SCOURGED, crowned with thorns, insulted and beaten, Jesus is made to carry the heavy weight of the cross on which he was to be crucified. As he walked along the road, the cross became heavier and heavier. Jesus must have felt at times that he could no longer keep going. Even when he fell, he made the effort to get up again and continue on the road. The crowd despised him, jeered him, cast insults at him. If only they had known who he was and what he was achieving by his suffering, resurrection to new life. But, no, they only saw a criminal, a loser, a reject, one cast out. Mary, his mother, accompanying Jesus on his way to crucifixion, also felt the weight of the cross as if it were on her own shoulders.

Addiction is a heavy cross, a cross that becomes heavier with time. Often you may think you can no longer keep going. The road to recovery is not a simple one, often three steps forward and two backwards. Going backwards is not to fail – the only failure is to give up trying. Not losing hope, you keep pushing yourself to struggle on, striving to reach each goal of recovery: resurrection to new life.

The weight of the cross of addiction falls even more heavily on the shoulders of your parents. They lie awake at night with worry. They wonder which will come first, recovery or death. They want to protect the other members of their family from the consequences of your addiction, while at the same time trying to support you, a balancing act which is often impossible. Your awareness of their suffering adds to the weight of the cross of addiction that you are carrying.

Like Jesus, you too feel the scorn and rejection of society. But those who despise you do not know who you are. They only see the addict, a loser, a reject, one cast out. They do not understand the path along which you struggle.

But at the end of the road, if you keep going, without losing hope and with the support of family or friends, there is resurrection to new life.

God, grant me the Serenity to accept my cross,
The Courage to change my life,
And the Wisdom to know your plan.

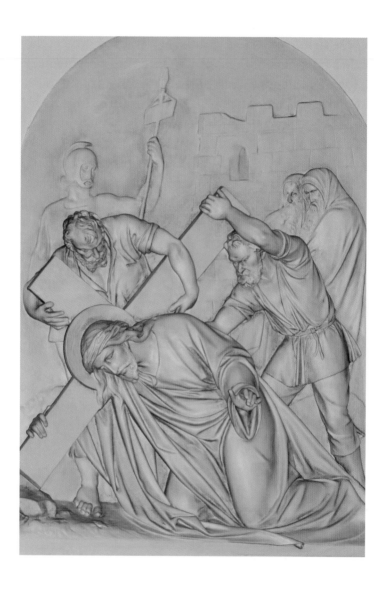

JESUS FALLS THE FIRST TIME

We Adore You, O Christ, and we Praise You –
because by Your Holy Cross, You have Redeemed the World.

Surely he has borne our infirmities and carried
our diseases; yet we accounted him stricken,
struck down by God and afflicted. But he was
wounded for our transgressions, crushed for
our iniquities, upon him was the punishment
that made us whole, and by his bruises we are
healed. He was oppressed and he was afflicted,
yet he did not open his mouth – like a sheep that
before its shearers is silent, so he did not open
his mouth.

Isaiah 53:4–7

Reflection by
H.E. ARCHBISHOP CHARLES BROWN
Apostolic Nuncio to Ireland

THE WEIGHT OF the cross that Jesus has been given to carry means that every step is difficult and every misstep becomes the occasion for a fall. Here before us in the Third Station, Jesus falls under the burden of the cross for the first time. There will be other missteps, other falls before he reaches the place of his crucifixion and Resurrection. This is only the first, but it reveals something very profound. Jesus is the New Adam, the firstborn of all creation (Col 1:15). It was Adam's fall, not physical but spiritual, that caused the damage to humanity which all of us, each in his or her own way, experience. Sin and death, suffering and sadness, addictions and afflictions – all of these are part of human experience as a result of what we call 'the fall' – the fall of our first parents from the condition of original blessedness which characterised creation at its radiant beginning.

In his passion, Jesus takes the burden of all that brokenness upon himself, and he carries it for us. In that sense, his fall, his first fall, is caused by Adam's fall, by Adam's turning away from God in disobedience and selfishness. It is that weight which makes Jesus collapse to the ground. But the remarkable thing about the Third Station of the Cross is that it is only the third. There are more to come. And that means that not only did Jesus fall, but that he also got up again and continued on.

When we think of people suffering from addiction, this station is immensely significant. In the first place, it makes us realise that addiction is but one manifestation of the wounded humanity that each and every one of us inherits. Our wounds take different forms. Not everyone suffers from addiction, but all of us are alike in our woundedness. The addicted person is no different from others. We are all wounded, and the Church, as Pope Francis reminds us, is a field hospital where all of us are in therapy. And, secondly, we see that Jesus fell and then got up and continued on. And so, we recognise that on the path to overcoming addiction there may be falls, missteps, setbacks. But there is always the possibility of getting up and continuing on. We can also be sure that when Jesus fell to the ground the first time in this Third Station, he was helped to get up. Surely a compassionate stranger, perhaps a pious Jewish person in Jerusalem, helped him struggle back to his feet. And isn't that true also with regard to addiction? It is with the help of others that those suffering from addiction rise again and move forward. Let us be generous and selfless in helping our brothers and sisters to walk again, and let us remember that the cross of Christ leads to resurrection.

God, grant me the Serenity to accept the falls in life,
The Courage to avoid those who cause my pain,
And the Wisdom to see the pitfalls.

JESUS MEETS HIS MOTHER

We Adore You, O Christ, and we Praise You –
because by Your Holy Cross, You have Redeemed the World.

When Jesus saw his mother and the disciple he loved standing beside her, he said to his mother, 'Woman here is your son,' then he said to the disciple, 'Here is your mother'.
John 19:26–7

Reflection by
KITTY, MOTHER OF AN ADDICT

MY SON HAS SUFFERED much over the years – he never really liked school and got involved with a group of friends who influenced him negatively. When he was a teenager he began to miss school and I suspected that he was smoking and drinking. My husband and I tried our best for him but at every chance he rebelled against us.

Reading the line 'this is your son' says everything that we ever said – we always knew, regardless of what happened, we had to stand by our son exactly because he was our son. Many people told us that we had to let him go and not worry about him but even though the advice was well meant, it was not something we felt we could do at that time.

Prayer was very important to me, especially as there were days that I felt I had no hope, times when I felt so alone. I worried for my son every day when he was not with us and I feared for what would happen to him. I prayed each day to Our Lady knowing that she had seen her son walk away from her burdened by his cross and was going in a direction that she couldn't understand.

When I found out my son was taking drugs my heart broke and we argued and he left. We didn't even have a phone number for him. When we finally got word that he was in custody, having been caught using,

I felt so relieved to hear that he was alive. When we spoke to him he blamed us for his troubles – this was very hard and it took a long time to understand that he was simply taking out his frustration on us.

Eventually my son went for addiction treatment – it took him some time to get close to the son we remember due to the trauma that he faced, but he did face it. He spoke to us recently and told us there was no place like home and this was the time that I knew he was back to himself.

I thank God for giving me my son and I am thankful for the strength to help my son through his difficulties.

God, grant all parents the Serenity to accept the trials that befall their children,

The Courage to stay strong and know your love for them,
And the Wisdom to know what to say.

SIMON HELPS JESUS CARRY HIS CROSS

We Adore You, O Christ, and we Praise You –
because by Your Holy Cross, You have Redeemed the World.

They compelled a passer-by, who was coming
in from the country, to carry his cross; it was
Simon of Cyrene, the father of Alexander and
Rufus.

Mark 15:21

Reflection by
ARCHBISHOP RICHARD CLARKE
Church of Ireland, Archbishop of Armagh

SIMON OF CYRENE takes up only a couple of verses of the Scriptures and yet he is, in his own way, one of the central figures in the story of the crucifixion. As Our Lord stumbles under the weight of the cross in his weakened state, having already been whipped and scourged. Simon is forced by the soldiers to carry the cross for Jesus. It must have been painful for Simon in every possible way. He certainly would not have chosen it for himself. Apart from the weight of the wooden beams of the cross, he would have been pushed and shoved by the soldiers, and perhaps even whipped. The passers-by might well have thought that Simon was the person being brought to crucifixion and they too would have mocked him, and jeered and spat at him. And yet there's a surprising footnote for us.

Simon of Cyrene is mentioned in the Gospel of Mark as 'the father of Alexander and Rufus'. This can surely only have been because those names were already known to the first readers of the Gospel, and we can reasonably infer from this that the family was part of the Christian community by the time the Gospel was written. May it not well have been that carrying the cross for Jesus was the first step on a road to discipleship for Simon of Cyrene, as he witnessed Christ's patient suffering for all humankind, and the total self-giving love that his crucifixion showed so fully?

Conquering addiction will always mean carrying a cross. It can never be easy. It would never be freely chosen. But, if we have the eyes to see it, 'the cross' may be the cross on which Christ was crucified, and by carrying it to Calvary for him, we are thereby in his company in a uniquely intimate and wonderful way. In God's grace, it might also mean that our example would enable others to carry their cross with ever-greater faith in the Christ who loves them too, and to the end of time.

God, grant me the Serenity to accept the cross of those I love,
The Courage to assist them through my care for them,
And the Wisdom to know when to offer help and when to simply pray for them.

VERONICA WIPES THE FACE OF JESUS

We Adore You, O Christ, and we Praise You —
because by Your Holy Cross, You have Redeemed the World.

The king will answer them, 'Truly I tell you, just as you did it to one of the least of these who are members of my family, you did it to me'.
Matthew 25:40

Reflection by
FR MICHAEL CONWAY
Pontifical University, Maynooth

IT IS EASY TO underestimate ordinary kindness. We can simply overlook the small, the incidental, and the minor. Yet, a modest gesture can mean everything, when someone is lost, or down and out, or trapped in a cycle of compulsion and addiction. Even a smile at the right time and in the right place can save! Veronica stands for all those small acts that comfort us, that encourage us, and that help us to change our lives for the better. Tradition has her wiping Jesus' face with a towel. In the background the mob is crying out for blood and destruction; but she steps out from the cowardly crowd and tends to someone in need. So often in our daily decisions, there is a faint whisper that adds to the common voice of the crowd. Veronica, however, invites us to take a different path: to be concerned for our neighbour, to be courageous, and to love in a tangible, concrete way. Little things do matter and can mean so much. At this station the small and the insignificant are given an eternal significance.

One of the greatest weaknesses of our time is indifference, indifference to the plight of others: the refugee, the homeless, the addict, the lost, the young, the despairing, the lonely and the elderly.

INDIFFERENCE

When Jesus came to Golgotha, they hanged him
on a tree,
They drove great nails through hands and feet,
and made a Calvary;
They crowned him with a crown of thorns, red
were his wounds and deep,
For those where crude and cruel days, and
human flesh was cheap.

When Jesus came to Birmingham they simply
passed him by,
They never hurt a hair of him, they only let him
die;
For men had grown more tender, and they
would not give him pain,
They only just passed down the street, and left
him in the rain.

Still Jesus cried, 'Forgive them, for they know
not what they do,'
And still it rained the wintry rain that drenched
him through and through
The crowds went home, and left the streets
without a soul to see,
And Jesus crouched against a wall and cried for
Calvary.

GA Studdert-Kennedy

As indifference and isolation are on the increase in our culture, small acts of kindness are so important in reminding us not only that we belong together, but also that we have the same fundamental needs, and that we ought to care for each other in the most ordinary of ways. Veronica stepped from the crowd and touched Jesus in his distress. Although, in the tradition, it is the towel that is left with an imprint of his face, it is her action that becomes the true reflection (*vera icona*) of what it is to follow him.

Lord, whenever I meet unhappiness, hurt, pain, prejudice, hatred and injustice, give me the wisdom and the courage to step from the crowd to respond in whatever way that I can.

God, grant me the Serenity to wash the tears from those who I love who are suffering,
The Courage to approach them with love,
And Wisdom to know the right time.

JESUS FALLS THE SECOND TIME

We Adore You, O Christ, and we Praise You —
because by Your Holy Cross, You have Redeemed the World.

Though he was in the form of God, Jesus did not
count equality with God a thing to be grasped,
he emptied himself, taking the form of a servant,
being born in the likeness of men.

Philippians 2:6–7

Reflection by
DAVID, FAMILY MEMBER OF AN ADDICT

IT IS DIFFICULT TO see the ones that we love fail and fall. How painful it must have been to see Jesus fall for the second time as he carried his cross, the weapon of his death. The pain that it must have caused him as he carried it with his already bruised and broken body. He had been through so much already, but his longest journey was yet to come. His pain was not yet over. How difficult it must have been to rise again and carry on, knowing that it was to only get worse, that his personal pain was not yet over.

The cross of addiction often brings life into total despair. It is not just the life of the addicted person that is affected but also the lives of their loved ones who want to help but can sometimes only watch as they struggle or fall under the pressure of their addiction.

As a loved one we want to help carry the cross, we want to take away the heavy burden and yet we know we can't. We have to watch the falls – the first, the second, and the ones that follow. As a son it was difficult to watch my father fall time and time again, and he fell so hard every time. It was painful to watch him pull down the ones he loved with him. My mother and my sisters and I were often the ones who were left to pick up the pieces, were left alone while he went to rehabilitation centres or even to prison. While he was away getting the help he needed we were the ones who had to fix what he had destroyed with his lies. He often used such places to escape, watching from afar as we tried to mend what he had broken – he was safe and we struggled. It was his Simons and his Veronicas who were hurt the most, and yet we loved him, and we knew that deep down he loved us too but his cross was heavy. There came a time when we could no longer be there when he got back up, when we had to disappear into the crowd. It doesn't mean we love him even less but sometimes it is not our cross to carry anymore.

It takes times for healing to happen. To acknowledge that wrong was done and that hurt was caused, for all to recognise that healing can take place. My father never wanted to take up his cross, and yet it is always there for him. My father loves us but sometimes it takes us a while to separate my father from his cross. To see his struggle, to see his pain is difficult but to see him as my father and not as an addict then all I can feel is love.

God, grant me Serenity when times are tough,
Courage to stay strong in difficult moments,
And Wisdom to know where to find help.

JESUS MEETS THE WOMEN OF JERUSALEM

We Adore You, O Christ, and we Praise You —
because by Your Holy Cross, You have Redeemed the World.

Jesus turned to them and said, 'Daughters of Jerusalem, do not weep for me; weep rather for yourselves and for your children. For look, the days are surely coming when people will say, 'Blessed are those who are barren, the wombs that have never borne children, the breasts that have never suckled!' Then they will begin to say to the mountains, 'Fall on us!'; to the hills, 'Cover us!' For if this is what is done to green wood, what will be done when the wood is dry?'

Luke 23:28–31

Reflection by
SR CONSILIO FITZGERALD
Founder: Cuan Mhuire

WHEN JESUS 'SET his face for Jerusalem'
(Lk 9:51) he knew well what lay ahead. Now it was
happening. Golgotha was perhaps one hundred metres
away.

The consequences of that rejection were now clear.
The women who had followed him wept when they
saw what had been done to him. His response was to
set aside his own appalling sufferings and to reach out
and comfort them.

His message went even deeper. Evil and sin are
a reality. Sin is the willful rejection of Jesus and his
message of love and forgiveness. Sin has consequences
for us as individuals. In our world today we also
see the consequences of evil and sin for countries.
Jesus was carrying the consequences of the sins of
humankind on his bruised shoulders. In a few short
years, the consequences unleashed by sin would
lead to the destruction of the Temple at the heart
of Jerusalem and to the slaughter of its women and
children.

To be a follower of Christ – to witness in our lives
to his message – is not about popularity. Nor is it about
standing weeping on the side lines. It's about putting,
in our actions, the needs and the sufferings of others
before our own. It's a mission of mercy to a broken
world. Its message heals. It brings fullness of life.

The road to recovery begins with the acceptance of our own powerlessness. There is great strength in this acceptance. It takes us beyond our own resources. It opens up our lives and relationships to healing. In accepting this suffering, all of the infinite goodness in Jesus was free to reach out to the women.

How often we feel bowed down by the weight of our addiction. It is always open to us to accept our powerlessness. With this acceptance comes the grace to understand our own goodness – the goodness which Jesus saw in the women of Jerusalem. Healing and recovery comes with expressing this goodness by reaching out, as he did, to others.

Families and friends experience that same sense of powerlessness in the face of the blindness of our addiction. The women of Jerusalem were good people. They wept as they saw Jesus pass by to the hill of Calvary. They watched as he went forward. Then they went home.

Families caught up in addiction do not have that option. There can be no standing aside from the realities of addictive behaviours.

Watching from the sidelines and weeping is not enough. It does not help the person in addiction. We are called to go beyond tears. That is why Cuan Mhuire, understanding their pain and fears, has always embraced families caught up by addiction and served them in real and practical ways, walking with them.

All of us are called to acknowledge the worries and fears of families and friends of individuals caught up in addiction. We are called to reach out to them, with empathy and understanding, as Jesus reached out to the women of Jerusalem.

God, grant me the Serenity to accept help from those who love me,
Courage to seek help from those who care for me,
And Wisdom to know who to trust.

JESUS FALLS THE THIRD TIME

We Adore You, O Christ, and we Praise You —
because by Your Holy Cross, You have Redeemed the World.

Our steps are made firm by the Lord, when he delights in our way; though we stumble, we shall not fall headlong, for the lord holds us by the hand.

Psalm 37:23–4

Reflection by
DAMIEN, AN ADDICT IN RECOVERY

I LEFT SCHOOL AT fifteen with no education. When I was seventeen I started taking ecstasy tablets and this gave me a false sense of confidence. This then escalated to being addicted to heroin, and my life totally changed as a person. When I was taking heroin, I did a lot of things that I regret and I ended up in prison. My wife left school at thirteen and she also got addicted to heroin. In 1996 my wife and I started a physeptone/methadone programme for six years. During this time, we had our first baby who, to our shame, was born addicted to methadone. Life on methadone was horrific – it was like being sedated all the time with no quality of life. There were so many times I wanted to stop taking methadone but if I didn't take it I would be in so much excruciating physical pain that my body would crave it. After many years of drug abuse, I was left a very broken person. In 2002 I was very suicidal and I lost the will to live. I was in so much physical and emotional pain I felt the only answer would be for me to kill myself and free myself from this pain.

Jesus fell under the weight of his heavy cross and I fell too. I believed that when I took my first drug I was throwing away my cross and trying to escape from all the difficulties in my life. Needless to say, drugs made it all so much worse. Then in 2002 a family member heard about a treatment centre in Knock, County Mayo called Community Cenacolo. In Cenacolo I learned how to live a normal life again with the healing power of Jesus in the Eucharist. I also learned how to carry my cross and when I fall to get back up again. Before Cenacolo my life was in total darkness. When I had a problem, I took drugs, but now when life gets difficult I pray to the risen Jesus and his Holy Mother for their help and they have never let me down. With the help of Cenacolo my life has been totally transformed. Every morning when I wake up I thank God for the gift of life and for all the beautiful people he has put in my life.

God, grant me the serenity to know that when I fall,
You will give me Courage to get back up,
This Wisdom will strengthen me for my journey.

JESUS IS STRIPPED OF HIS GARMENTS

We Adore You, O Christ, and we Praise You —
because by Your Holy Cross, You have Redeemed the World.

Then Jesus said, 'Father forgive them; for they
do not know what they are doing'. And they cast
lots to divide his clothing.
Luke 23:34

Reflection by
FR MICHAEL MCCULLAGH CM

PEOPLE WHO HAVE been victims of addiction, and especially those who have had to make the streets of our cities their home, speak of being so vulnerable, of being called the nastiest names imaginable and even of being spat at. There is no hiding place.

Everything that gave them dignity up until then had been taken from them. Yes, they were stripped of everything. In our Christian tradition, it is so hard to understand that we have a God, who in Jesus, stood naked before the world. This is what we see in the Tenth Station on the Way of the Cross.

I once remember a man, called Tom, in Sing-Sing prison in New York, say, 'I feel Jesus Christ in my bones, he has HIV/AIDS today.' Everything that once gave Tom dignity – clothes, well-being, good health, and people who once had some regard for him – was now taken away. Yet, he knew that Jesus too had that experience of being stripped of everything. Somehow, he believed that Christ now lived in his nakedness.

On the graduation days in Camino Treatment Centre in Enfield those who have found recovery look good, their bodies renewed and their eyes clear. It is as if they were clothed anew. Echoes of the baptismal ceremony return as they receive their christening robe, 'See in this outward garment, the sign of your inward dignity'.

Those of us who often stand helplessly by, or are pushed aside, by our loved ones, friends and those known to us in addiction, would desire deeply to clothe them with the comforting garment of reassurance, of acceptance, of tough love and, above all, healing. Jesus did say, 'I was naked and you clothed me'. If Jesus Christ is in the bones of those stripped of dignity, as with Tom in that prison, naked to stares and harsh judgments, then we are placing the garment of comfort on his fragile body. In embracing people like Tom, we are embracing Christ himself.

Lord, I make two requests today. Help me to see with new eyes, to find you in those who have been stripped of all dignity. Secondly, I ask that my sisters and brothers will today come to the awareness that Christ is naked in them, and that they may allow us to robe them with the garment of Christian dignity once more.

God, grant me serenity when I feel like my dignity is being stripped,
The Courage to face my trials with strength,
And the Wisdom to know that Your plan is greater than my trials.

THE CRUCIFIXION – JESUS IS NAILED TO THE CROSS

We Adore You, O Christ, and we Praise You –
because by Your Holy Cross, You have Redeemed the World.

The people stood by, watching; but the leaders
scoffed at him saying, 'He saved others; let him
save himself if he is the Messiah of God, his
chosen one'. The soldiers also mocked him,
coming up and offering him sour wine, and
saying 'If you are the King of the Jews, save
yourself!'

Luke 23:35–7

Reflection by
SR STAN KENNEDY
Founder: Focus Ireland

LET US VISUALISE the terrible sight of the crucifixion. Jesus, being stripped of his garments, was violently thrown upon the cross and his hands and feet nailed thereto.

We could try to feel within us the excruciating pain Jesus would have experienced. Even in such excruciating pain we see Jesus calm, peaceful and silent. He has such spiritual stamina and determination to fulfil the Father's will, that he was able to endure the pain without blaming, cursing, trying to escape or walk out making compromises.

His major crime, according to those who crucified him, is that he claimed to be the son of God, and that he also preached that we are also children of God, having the same nature as God though we are not conscious of it. He came to awaken in us our true selves as divine. It is for this that he endured all this physical and emotional pain. He allows his body, along with it his own personal plans, desires and the reasoning of his rational mind, to be nailed to the cross. In other words, he has surrendered himself totally to the will of the father, so that he could be in communion with his heavenly father, the source of life, the cosmic wisdom.

We are struggling with this terrible sickness of chemical or non-chemical addictions. There are many causes for this. This is a crucifixion in itself.

People who have addictions need acceptance, kindness and different kinds of support and professional help. For people with faith recognising the support of God (and surrendering to God) is crucial for them and also for their families. This, the path of surrender to the God of one's understanding, is found to be most beneficial and the easiest option for addicts. It is a 'letting go' of the old ways and accepting life as it comes. It is surrendering of one's ego, desires and mind's habit mechanism through systematic and regular introspection. The path of surrender means learning to forgive, developing faith in God's goodness and a positive attitude to life. Training the mind to be completely in the present opens up a new consciousness. Then we are at one with Jesus as he was with the Father at the time of his crucifixion.

God, grant me the Serenity of feeling Your presence at my lowest moments,
The Courage to face up to my vice,
And the Wisdom to know that I am loved.

JESUS DIES ON THE CROSS

We Adore You, O Christ, and we Praise You —
because by Your Holy Cross, You have Redeemed the World.

From noon on, darkness came over the whole
land until three in the afternoon. And about
three o'clock Jesus cried with a loud voice 'Eli,
Eli, lema sabachthani' that is, 'My God, my God,
why have you forsaken me? – then Jesus cried
again with a loud voice and breathed his last.

Matthew 27:45–50

Reflection by
FR ADRIAN CROWLEY
Cenacolo Ireland, Knock

WHEN WE REFLECT on this scene we see our Lord dying on a cross, the bitterest experience.

It says to us 'I am with you even in the worst moment' – we are never abandoned by God. We may have left the right path, we may have said no to wisdom. When our parents and friends warned us to be careful, we nodded and said yes but then we went and did as we wanted. We strayed but God always accepts us back, always forgives.

By means of the cross, God lifts our burdens and washes away our sins. He gives us new life, a new chance, no matter how often we fall – he lifts us up and sets us on our feet again. What should we do? Simply surrender to his care!

We cannot do it alone but with God we can – Jesus is eternally faithful.

We pray,
I adore you holy cross, covered and tinted with
the precious blood of our Saviour,
I adore you, my God – placed on the cross for
me,
I adore you, holy cross – for love of the one who
is my Lord.

God, grant me Serenity in my transition,
The Courage to follow through,
And Wisdom to know that You are near.

JESUS IS TAKEN DOWN FROM THE CROSS

We Adore You, O Christ, and we Praise You —
because by Your Holy Cross, You have Redeemed the World.

Joseph of Arimathea, who was a disciple of Jesus, though a secret one because of his fear of the Jews, asked Pilate to let him take the body of Jesus. Pilate gave him permission; so he came and removed his body.

John 19:38

Reflection by
FR DAVID SONGI
President: St Luke Institute

MARY STOOD SILENTLY with the apostle John, entrusted to her by Jesus, and watched three men labour to remove her son's body from the cross. At first her eyes overflowed with tears of grief, but then she gazed on the other two crosses: two thieves who had spoken to Jesus right before he died. How her son loved them! She knew. Unable to avoid repeated crimes and condemned by the world, they were now free. Several men and women stood near them, weeping for the husbands, fathers, brothers they could not save from death. Mary prayed with them.

The two men on the crosses on each side of Jesus are not unlike those men and women who suffer from addiction and experience hopelessness. The words of Christ, 'Today, you will be with me in Paradise!' address all people in despair, especially those bound to the cross of addiction, powerlessness over alcohol, drugs, gambling, pornography, sex and other compulsive behaviours. The families and friends gathered around the cross of addiction take courage at these words of Christ, placing the apparently lifeless bodies of their loved ones into a treatment programme, where they wait patiently, as Mary confidently awaited the Resurrection.

Mary is a powerful symbol of the Church, standing beside the bodies of those who experience suffering and death, and weeping with understanding, compassion and hope. This love also touches the families and friends of people caught up in addiction. Like the families of those gathered on Calvary, gazing on the bodies of their beloved, and agonising over their powerlessness to help them, those people closest to addicts experience tremendous frustration and see no clear path to help them. Knowing they are not alone is so helpful! Having an ally who can sincerely hope in the face of suffering and death is a true gift.

Merciful God, hear the prayers of all who stand around the cross, mourning the losses they have witnessed in the addictions of their loved ones. Grant them the hope offered to them by Christ and his Church. May the Holy Spirit touch and heal the wounds of every broken family.

God, grant me the Serenity to accept my weakness,
The Courage to follow through with treatment,
And the Wisdom to know that I am loved by God
regardless of my cross.

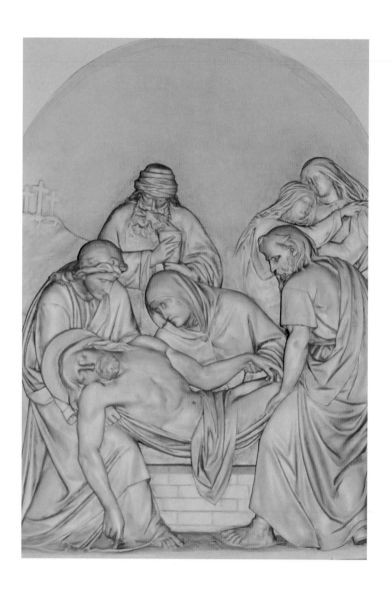

JESUS IS LAID IN THE TOMB

We Adore You, O Christ, and we Praise You –
because by Your Holy Cross, You have Redeemed the World.

Then Joseph brought a linen cloth, and taking
down the body, wrapped it in the linen cloth,
and laid it in the tomb that had been hewn out
of the rock. He then rolled a stone against the
door of the tomb. Mary Magdalene and Mary the
mother of Jesus saw where the body was laid.

Mark 15:46–7

Reflection by
LUCY, A SOUP RUN VOLUNTEER

I HAVE SEEN MANY people who have come to our service looking for help – in many ways they are in their tomb. I sometimes wonder what they are thinking. I can become so caught up in my own judgements and ideas that the reality of the situation these people face passes me by.

The tomb that Jesus lay in was cold, it was dark, it was empty to the human eye and yet it was the link room between heaven and earth. The tomb where Jesus rested was a doorway through which God's plan would be fully revealed to the world. The tomb where Jesus lay was not regarded as a sacred place and yet we know that there rested the saviour of the world.

When I look at those who we serve I sometimes ask myself 'why?' Why are these people suffering? The difficulty about these questions is that we will never fully understand the suffering of others – we can never fully understand the decisions that they make but we must be assured of God's love, present in every situation. I am aware that often God works through my life and sometimes all I can do is offer a smile or a kind word or a warm drink.

Having grown up with an addict I can understand the suffering that the families go through – the heartache of knowing that strangers are looking after their loved ones – but I also know that sometimes loved ones just cannot offer the support that a stranger can; shame and pride are part of the struggle of addiction. Anonymity is part of the healing process and unfortunately part of the human condition is to look upon those closest to us with suspicion.

Often we talk about addicts needing to hit rock bottom before seeking help – the tomb is a symbol of rock bottom and yet it is also our great symbol of hope. The tomb is where God's mercy is most evident and it is the place where the stark truths of life become real. My prayer is that we can all look with trust to God who, even in our tomb, is present and working in ways that we will never understand.

God, grant me the Serenity to retreat and accept help in my distress,
Courage to acknowledge that I am buried under the weight of my pain,
And Wisdom to know that I have many supports that I can reach out to.

Sara Kyne

THE RESURRECTION – JESUS RISES FROM THE DEAD

We Adore You, O Christ, and we Praise You –
because by Your Holy Cross, You have Redeemed the World.

The angel said to the women, 'do not be afraid;
I know that you are looking for Jesus who was
crucified. He is not here; for he has risen as he
said. Come, see the place where he lay. Then
go quickly and tell his disciples – He has been
raised from the dead.'

Matthew 28:5–7

Reflection by
ARCHBISHOP EAMON MARTIN
Catholic Archbishop of Armagh

'DO NOT BE afraid. He is risen!' The angel's words to the women on that first Easter morning echo down the centuries to our own day, confronting our fears, offering hope for this new day and for tomorrow. 'Go quickly and tell the others,' the angel continued, as if to say, 'Don't keep this Good News to yourself!'

Sometimes when you hear of people who have gone for help with addiction and come back with their health restored and life back on track, you might think – not me; my life is beyond redemption. But do not be afraid. If you are willing to let go and open yourself up to the grace of God, you too can learn how to hope again. You may have made a mess of things. You may have lost control of your life. You've hurt family and friends. BUT YOU ARE NOT DEFINED BY YOUR ADDICTION! The good within you is longing to get out!

The long and dark Good Friday gave way to a joyful Easter Day! Step by step, day by day, recovery and renewal are possible. Come and see. Swallow pride, take an honest look at life. Waken up out of the darkness that has been smothering your goodness and potential. Learn to live again!

Good people, real friends, do not give up on you. Thank God for them. They are the angels in your life who pick you up again and again. They believe in you –

no matter what. Should you decide to enter recovery, they will be there for you today, tomorrow, the next day … through all the meetings, aftercare, relapses and fresh starts. They will help you avoid the people, places and things that might drag you down and set you back.

Go quickly. Tell someone you're ready to begin the journey home to the person you really are. Do not be afraid. Jesus is walking beside you. He will not abandon you. He is risen!

God, grant me the Serenity to know that better day's lie ahead,
The Courage to accept help so that I might reach them,
And the Wisdom to accept all the assistance I need.

━ USEFUL ORGANISATIONS ━

The following organisations are acknowledged for their work in the area of addiction treatment and social justice issues.

Capuchin Day Centre, Dublin

The Capuchin Day Centre was established in 1969 by Br Kevin Crowley, and he has journeyed with people in need since then. Providing breakfast and lunch facilities, the centre also offers food parcels to an increasing number of recipients each week. The centre provides a medical service, chiropody clinics, an optical service together with advice and information clinics.

Peter McVerry Trust

Father Peter McVerry has been working with Dublin's young homeless for more than thirty years. In 1974 Fr McVerry moved to Summerhill, in Dublin's north inner city, where he witnessed first-hand the problems of homelessness and deprivation. In 1983 he founded

The Arrupe Society, a charity to provide housing and support for young homeless people as a response to the growing numbers experiencing homelessness in Dublin. Today the Peter McVerry Trust offers a wide variety of housing and addiction treatment services to those who seek assistance.

Cuan Mhuire

Cuan Mhuire is a charitable drug, alcohol and gambling rehabilitation organisation in Ireland. Cuan Mhuire offers a comprehensive, structured, abstinence based residential programme to persons suffering from alcohol, other chemical dependencies and gambling addictions. Cuan Mhuire was founded by Sr Consilio Fitzgerald, a member of the Sisters of Mercy in 1966. Cuan Mhuire has its own programme, developed by Sr Consilio and her staff over a period of fifty years, and has rehabilitation centres and other facilities all over Ireland, both north and south dealing with approximately two thousand five hundred people each year.

Cenacolo Community

The Community was founded by an Italian nun, Mother Elvira Petrozzi, in 1983. For many years, she had been concerned by the destruction she had seen among people of all ages through drug abuse and she longed to help them. Today there are houses worldwide with over two thousand men and women in the programme. The house for men in Ireland was opened in Knock, Co. Mayo in 1999. While secular programmes will use methadone and other drug substitutes to wean people off drugs, Mother Elvira has a completely different approach. She believes in showing addicts a better life. She encourages them to find out who they are and to face up to their difficulties. They discover a God who loves them. They learn to accept a simple lifestyle and rediscover the gifts of work, friendship and of faith in the Word of God, instead of relying on the crutch of drugs to escape from everything that is too painful to deal with.

Camino Network, Enfield

The St James Camino network is a charity dedicated to rehabilitating and supporting drug-dependent men living in Ireland. Since 1997 it has run holistic residential programmes for those who have shown an initial commitment to achieving a drug-free existence – without the barrier of high cost. In that time the network has delivered a new start to the lives of over five hundred participants and their families from all walks of life.

Focus Ireland

In 1985 Sr Stan Kennedy established Focus Point (now Focus Ireland) on Eustace Street, Dublin. The organisation provided street work services to young people, advice, advocacy, information and help with finding a home as well as a warm welcoming place to meet and have a low-cost meal. Since its foundation Focus Ireland has continued to grow and its research and advocacy work ensures that the rights of people who are homeless remain on the political agenda. In addition to its Dublin projects, it now has services and housing projects across Ireland, including Waterford, Kilkenny, Cork, Sligo and Limerick.

St Luke Institute

St Luke Institute is an internationally renowned Catholic education and treatment centre dedicated to healthy life and ministry for clergy and religious men and women around the globe through assessments, treatment and education.